Events of 1961

News for the year

Cdr Alan Shepard, the first American in space, and his wife Louise, left, meet US President Kennedy and his wife Jackie with Vice-President Lyndon Johnson at the White House, 8 May 1961.

By Hugh Morrison

MONTPELIER PUBLISHING

Front cover (clockwise from left): US President John F Kennedy and British Prime Minister Harold Macmillan meet for talks in Bermuda, 21 December. Yuri Gagarin, the first man in space, 12 April. The Berlin Wall, built 13 April. The US First Lady, Jackie Kennedy.

Back cover (clockwise from top): Ken doll launched 11 March. Astronaut Alan Shepard splashes down, 5 May. The Jaguar E type, launched 3 April. The farthing, withdrawn 1 January. The British liner SS *Canberra*, launched 2 June. Guildford Cathedral, consecrated 17 May. Top Cat, first shown 27 September.

Image credits: Cecil W Staughton, Andrew Bone, Retroplum, Nobel Foundation, Russell Trebor, McFadden Publications, Pierre Stromberg, *New York World Telegram and Sun*, Guy Villeminot, Wasforgas, David Shankbone, Harman AG, Flagstaff Fotos, Pressens Bild, Dutch National Archive/Anefo, NASA, Michael Vaslaty, Purple, C5813, JFK Library, Psych Art, Andrew Hurley, Arpingstone, Hinnerk Rümenapf, John Matthew Smith, Jac de Nijs, Harry Pot, Peter Heinz Junge, US Army, National Gallery, 8474tim, Hanna Barbera, Michael and Willy Finder, Lynn Gilbert, German Federal Archives, US Army, Jac de Nijs/Anefo, David Shankbone, Nic Redhead, Rob Gaston, National Library of Australia, Israel Government Press Office, Robert Knudsen.

Published by Montpelier Publishing.
Printed and distributed by Amazon KDP.
This edition © 2020. All rights reserved.
ISBN: 9798691570896

January 1961

Sunday 1: Britain's farthing coin, one quarter of an old penny, ceases to be legal tender.

Australia becomes the second country after the USA to allow the sale of contraceptive pills.

Bingo halls are legalised in the UK.

The farthing, Britain's smallest coin, ceases to be legal tender.

Monday 2: Actor Neil Dudgeon (DCI Barnaby in *Midsomer Murders*) is born in Doncaster, England.

Tuesday 3: The US Embassy in Cuba closes as diplomatic relations are broken off between the two countries.

Finland's worst aeroplane crash takes place near Vaasa with 25 people killed.

Wednesday 4: East Germany's government holds crisis talks about the large numbers of its citizens leaving for the west, with the first plans discussed for the building of the Berlin Wall.

Austrian physicist Erwin Schrödinger, famous for his particle-physics analogy known as Schrödinger's Cat, dies aged 73.

January 1961

Thursday 5: Italian sculptor Alfredo Fioraventi admits he forged the famous archaeological finds known as the Etruscan Terracotta Warriors.

Dashiell Hammett dies on 10 January.

Friday 6: John F Kennedy is formally elected as 35th President of the United States by the Electoral College.

Saturday 7: Five African countries form the Casablanca Group, a NATO type organisation.

The action series *The Avengers* is first broadcast on British TV.

Sunday 8: In a French referendum, citizens vote 75% in favour of independence for the colony of Algeria.

Monday 9: The British government announces the breakup of the Portland Spy Ring, a network of Soviet 'sleeper' agents operating in Britain, including a respectable married couple living in a suburban bungalow in Ruislip, Middlesex.

Tuesday 10: American 'pulp fiction' detective author Dashiell Hammett, creator of the character Sam Spade, dies aged 66.

Soviet 'sleeper agent' Peter Kroger, living undercover in a house near London (left) is caught on 9 January.

January 1961

The Supremes, with Diana Ross (centre) sign their first record contract on 15 January.

Wednesday 11: Karl von Habsburg, eldest son of the last Crown Prince of Austro-Hungary, is born in Starmberg, West Germany.

Thursday 12: British actor and, historian Simon Russell Beale is born in Penang, Malaya.

Friday 13: Graham McPherson, better known as 'Suggs', lead singer of the band Madness, is born in Hastings, England.

Saturday 14: The football players' union of England and Wales threatens to go on strike if maximum wage caps of £20 per game are not lifted. Shortly afterwards the cap is dropped and the era of huge salaries begins.

Sunday 15: The Supremes sign their first recording contract with Motown Records.

Monday 16: The USA bans travel by its citizens to Cuba.

Iowa bank clerk Mrs Burnice Geiger is arrested for embezzlement and is later found to have stolen $2.12m, the largest theft of its kind in US history.

Tuesday 17: Outgoing US President Dwight D Eisenhower makes his farewell TV address.

Wednesday 18: The closest general election in history takes place when Zanzibar's Afro-Shirazi party wins by a margin of one vote.

January 1961

English footballer Peter Beardsley MBE is born in Hexham, Northumberland.

Thursday 19: A Mexican DC-8 airliner crashes in a blizzard near New York and bursts into flames; all but 4 of the 106 people on board survive.

Friday 20: New US President John F Kennedy takes the Oath of Office, which is broadcast on colour television for the first time.

Saturday 21: The nuclear submarine USS *George Washington*, completes a record 66-day underwater patrol.

Sunday 22: European Freemasonry groups sign the Strasbourg Appeal for mutual co-operation.

President Kennedy.

Monday 23: A group of Portuguese radicals seize control of the cruise ship *Santa Maria*, taking 940 people hostage.

Tuesday 24: A nuclear explosion is narrowly avoided when a B52 bomber armed with two hydrogen bombs crashes near Goldsboro, North Carolina.

Actress Marilyn Monroe is divorced from playwright Arthur Miller.

The USS *George Washington*.

January 1961

Wednesday 25: John F Kennedy holds the first live televised Presidential press conference.

Walt Disney's animated film *101 Dalmations* premieres in St Petersburg, Florida.

Thursday 26: Janet G Travell becomes the first woman to be appointed as personal physician to a US President.

Friday 27: Following the failure of a ventilation seal, the Soviet submarine *S-80* sinks with the loss of all 68 crew in the Barents Sea; its wreckage is not discovered until 1968.

Ham the Chimp.

Saturday 28: Malcolm X (Malcolm Little) of the black supremacist group the Nation of Islam meets secretly with representatives of the Ku Klux Klan to discuss the prevention of racial integration.

Sunday 29: Communist-controlled North Vietnam announces the formation of the paramilitary group the Viet Cong, dedicated to the overthrow of capitalism in South Vietnam.

Monday 30: US President Kennedy approves a $41 million military aid package to counteract communist insurgency in South Vietnam.

Tuesday 31: Ham the Chimp makes a successful test space flight in NASA's Mercury *Redstone 2* rocket, returning to Earth safely after a 16 minute sub-orbital trip.

February 1961

Wednesday 1: The first push-button telephones go into use in the USA.

Marilyn Monroe's final film, *The Misfits*, is released in the USA; it is also the final film of Monroe's co-star Clark Gable.

The Western Electric 1500 is the first push-button telephone to go into use on 1 February.

Thursday 2: The parents of US President Barack Obama, Barack Obama Sr and Stanley Ann Durham are married in Hawaii.

Friday 3: The first Boeing EC135, known as a 'doomsday plane' takes off. Intended to act as a US mobile command centre in the event of nuclear war, at least one such plane is kept airborne at all times until the fall of the USSR in 1991.

Saturday 4: A nationalist uprising begins in the Portuguese colony of Angola.

Sunday 5: Film star Marilyn Monroe is voluntarily admitted to a psychiatric hospital in New York under a pseudonym.

Britain's *Sunday Telegraph* newspaper is first published.

February 1961

Marilyn Monroe and Clark Gable in The Misfits.

Monday 6: Seven senior executives from General Electric and Westinghouse are jailed for rigging bids in government contracts.

Tuesday 7: George Low, head of NASA, submits his plan for a manned moon landing to US President John F Kennedy.

Wednesday 8: US President John F Kennedy causes a stir when he mispronounces the name of Canada's Prime Minister, John Diefenbaker, several times during a press conference.

Vince Neil, lead singer of Mötley Crüe, is born in Hollywood, California.

Thursday 9: The Beatles perform at the Cavern Club, Liverpool, for the first time.

Friday 10: The world's largest hydroelectric power station to this date, opens at Lewiston, New York, using water from Niagara Falls to generate 2.4 gigawatts of power per hour.

Saturday 11: Residents of British Cameroon hold a referendum, voting to split the country between the newly independent states of Nigeria and the former French Republic of Cameroon.

February 1961

The mysterious 'Coso Artifact' is found in California on 13 February.

Sunday 12: The USSR launches the *Venera 1* space probe towards Venus, although radio contact is lost before it reaches the planet.

Monday 13: Prospectors in California find a strange manufactured metal object buried within what is thought to be a 500,000 year old piece of rock. Known as the 'Coso Artifact', it is later proven by experts to be a 1920s spark plug encased over decades by natural concretion.

Tuesday 14: The 103rd element, Lawrencium, is synthesised by a team of scientists at the University of Berkeley, California.

Wednesday 15: 72 people including the entire USA figure skating team is killed when Sabena Flight 548 crashes near Brussels, Belgium.

Thursday 16: The American satellite *Explorer 9* is launched into orbit.

Friday 17: The silent film 'vamp' actress Nita Naldi (*Dr Jekyll and Mr Hyde*) dies aged 66.

Soviet stamp commemorating *Venera 1*.

February 1961

The Action for Life protest of 18 February.

Saturday 18: 5000 demonstrators led by the pacifist philosopher Bertrand Russell stage a 'sit-in' at the Ministry of Defence in London, in protest over Britain's nuclear programme.

Sunday 19: A seven year old boy, Harry Stage, is rescued after falling 275 feet down a well in Arizona; miraculously he sustains only two broken legs and a broken pelvis.

Monday 20: British actress Imogen Stubbs is born in Rothbury, Northumberland.

Tuesday 21: UN Security Council Resolution 161 is approved, authorising military force to prevent civil war in the Congo.

Frederick M Jones, founder of Thermo King refrigerated transport, dies aged 68.

Wednesday 22: Neil Simon's first play, *Come Blow Your Horn*, premieres on Broadway.

The playwright Neil Simon, who goes on to write *The Odd Couple* and *Barefoot in the Park*.

Thursday 23: British explorer Duncan Carse travels to the uninhabited Antarctic island of South Georgia for an 18 month solo trip; he loses most of his

February 1961

supplies during a storm in May and is finally rescued in September. Despite the setbacks, Carse's research was invaluable during the 1982 Falklands War.

Friday 24: The body of former Hungarian Prime Minister Imre Nagy, executed for his part in the 1956 uprising against the Soviets, is removed by Soviet authorities from its tomb and reburied in a secret location not revealed until 1989.

Saturday 25: Pilot Paul Bikle sets the world altitude record for a glider at 46,266 feet (14,102 metres).

Imre Nagy.

The last tram service ends in Sydney, Australia.

Sunday 26: King Mohammed V of Morocco dies aged 51 and is succeeded by his son, Hassan II.

Monday 27: Professor Henry Kissinger, 37, future US Secretary of State, is appointed a consultant to the National Security Agency.

Tuesday 28: This date marks the beginning of the Vietnam Era; any US service person who served in Vietnam between this day and 7 May 1975 is classified as a Vietnam veteran.

Henry Kissinger.

March 1961

Wednesday 1: The Peace Corps, the US voluntary service organisation, is established.

Thursday 2: Algerian nationalists agree to peace talks with French colonial authorities after seven years of conflict.

Artist Pablo Picasso, 79, marries Jacquelin Rocque, 35.

Friday 3: A London shop assistant, Elsie May Batten, is murdered by 21 year old Edwin Bush, who becomes the first criminal to be caught by the Identikit facial description system.

Saturday 4: 20,000 people watch a reenactment of the inauguration of President Lincoln on the event's centenary; twice as many as those who attended the original event.

Sunday 5: The US Air Force announces the development of an atomic clock accurate to one second in 1271 years.

Monday 6: The British singer, ukelele player and actor George Formby dies aged 56.

Singer George Formby, shown here in 1940, dies on 6 March.

March 1961

Tuesday 7: USAF Captain Robert White becomes the first person to travel faster than Mach 4, flying at 2,905 mph in an X-15 aeroplane.

Wednesday 8: The first US Polaris nuclear submarines arrive in the UK and are greeted by protestors at Scotland's Holy Loch.

Sir Thomas Beecham, founder of the London Philharmonic and Royal Philharmonic orchestras, dies aged 81.

Thursday 9: The USSR launches *Sputnik 9*, containing a test dummy cosmonaut 'Ivan Ivanovich'.

Friday 10: The USA's Jet Propulsion Laboratory bounces a radio signal off the planet Venus, which makes the 35 million mile round trip back to Earth in just over six minutes.

Saturday 11: The 'Ken' doll, boyfriend to 'Barbie', is launched by the Mattel toy company in the USA.

Sunday 12: Pakistan's Mushtaq Mohammed, 17, becomes the youngest cricketer to score a Test century, a record which remains unbroken for 40 years.

Monday 13: Cyprus joins the British Commonwealth.

Tuesday 14: The New Testament of the New English Bible is published. A fully revised version based on the oldest surviving texts, it is released on the 350th anniversary of the publication of the King James Bible.

Barbie's boyfriend Ken is launched on March 1961.

March 1961

Spartacus, starring Kirk Douglas, wins Best Film.

Wednesday 15: South Africa announces its withdrawal from the British Commonwealth due to criticism of its apartheid regime.

Thursday 16: *Spartacus* wins Best Film in the 18th Golden Globe Awards.

The Disney comedy film *The Absent Minded Professor* starring Fred McMurray is released in the USA.

Friday 17: Albert de Salvo is arrested for housebreaking in Boston, Massachusetts. Jailed for a year, he is later caught again and revealed as the serial killer nicknamed the 'Boston Strangler'.

Saturday 18: Luxembourg wins the Eurovision Song Contest with *Nous les Amoureux* sung by Jean-Claude Pascal.

Sunday 19: 250 people are killed when a series of tornadoes hits East Pakistan (now Bangladesh).

Left: Jean-Claude Pascal, winner of the Eurovision Song Contest.

March 1961

Monday 20: John Clark Gable is born in the same hospital in which his film star father Clark Gable died four months earlier.

Tuesday 21: The Beatles (with Stuart Sutcliffe on drums) begin a regular schedule at Liverpool's Cavern Club, which lasts for 300 performances and catapults them to fame.

Wednesday 22: Following his retirement as US President, Dwight D Eisenhower returns to his former occupation of army officer, accepting a commission as a five star general.

Thursday 23: Major Lawrence R Bailey Jr, USAF, becomes the first prisoner of war of the Vietnam era when his plane crash-lands in Laos.

Friday 24: NASA launches its Mercury-Redstone trial space rocket using a test dummy.

NASA officials with the Mercury-Redstone rocket.

Saturday 25: The USSR launches a second test dummy rocket, Sputnik 10.

Sunday 26: France defeats Wales 8-6 to win the Five Nations rugby tournament.

March 1961

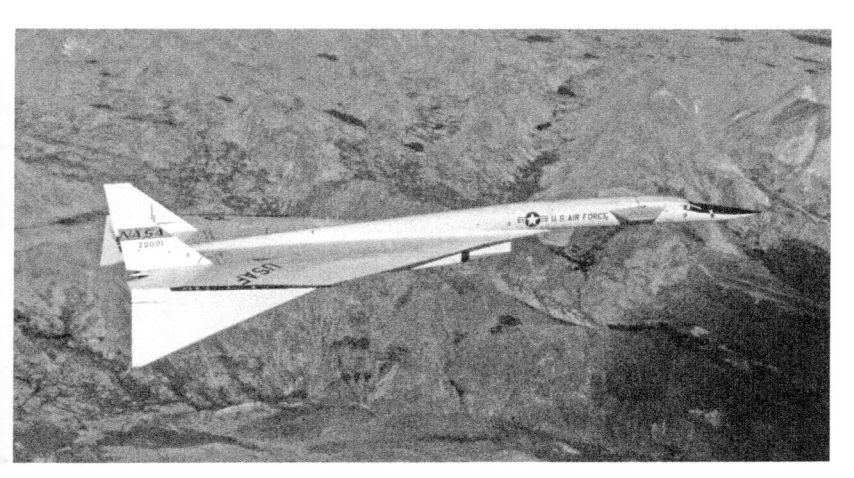

The USAF/NASA prototype B-70 bomber in flight.

Monday 27: Ian Fleming's ninth James Bond novel, *Thunderball* is published.

Nine black students stage a 'read in' at the whites-only section of a segregated public library in Jackson, Mississipi.

Tuesday 28: The USA cancels the development of its B-70 Valkyrie nuclear powered aeroplane.

Wednesday 29: The 23rd Amendment to the Constitution of the United States is ratified, allowing residents of Washington, DC (which is classed as a district, not a state) to vote in presidential elections.

Thursday 30: The Single Convention on Narcotic Drugs goes into effect, banning the distribution of certain harmful drugs in a number of countries.

Friday 31: The Republic of Ireland's Cork, Bandon and South Coast railway closes after 112 years of operation.

April 1961

Saturday 1: The first TV commercials are broadcast in New Zealand.

Scottish singer Susan Boyle is born in Blackburn, West Lothian.

Sunday 2: Australia's Janice Andrew sets the world record women's 100 metres swimming time (butterfly stroke) at 1.08.9 in Tokyo.

Susan Boyle.

Monday 3: Comedian and actor Eddie Murphy is born in Brooklyn, New York.

Leadbetter's Possum, believed to have become extinct in 1909, is re-discovered in Australia.

The Jaguar E-Type sports car is launched in Britain.

Tuesday 4: US President John F. Kennedy approves the military's plans for invasion of communist-held Cuba via the Bay of Pigs.

Eddie Murphy.

April 1961

The E-Type Jaguar is launched on 3 April.

Wednesday 5: Singer Barbra Streisand makes her TV debut on *Tonight Starring Jack Paar.*

Thursday 6: The Governor of New York, Nelson Rockefeller, approves plans for the construction of the World Trade Center.

Friday 7: English artist Vanessa Bell, a member of the 'Bloomsbury Group' and sister of Virginia Woolf, dies aged 81.

Saturday 8: 238 people are killed when the British passenger ship MV *Dara* explodes off the coast of Dubai, in what is thought to be a terrorist attack, although no group claims responsibility.

Barbra Streisand makes her TV debut on 5 April.

Sunday 9: The last Los Angeles streetcar service ends.

The exiled King Zog I of Albania dies in Paris aged 65.

Monday 10: NASA makes the first accurate radar measurement of the distance between Earth and Venus (26,372,600 miles).

Britain's William P Sidney (Viscount De L'Isle) becomes Governor-General of Australia.

April 1961

Yuri Gagarin, first man in space.

Tuesday 11: The trial of senior Nazi Adolf Eichmann begins in Jerusalem.

Wednesday 12: Yuri Gagarin of the USSR becomes the first man in space when he is launched into orbit from Kazakhstan in the *Vostok 1* rocket.

Thursday 13: An attempted military coup against the Salazar regime in Portugal is unsuccessful.

Friday 14: The American Standards Association approves the size of metal shipping containers, now used worldwide.

Returning cosmonaut Yuri Gagarin receives a hero's welcome in Red Square, Moscow.

Saturday 15: The US invasion of Cuba begins, as eight US aircraft attack Cuban airfields.

Sunday 16: Britain's Stirling Moss wins the Vienna Grand Prix in a Lotus 18.

Monday 17: Exiled Cuban forces with US sea and air support land at the Bay of Pigs in Cuba at 01.00.

Burt Lancaster wins the Academy Award for Best Actor for *Elmer Gantry* and Elizabeth Taylor wins Best Actress for *Butterfield 8*.

Tuesday 18: Cuban troops push back the US-supported invasion force, which suffers heavy losses.

Wednesday 19: 1,189 US-supported Cuban troops are captured as the invasion of Cuba ends in failure.

April 1961

Thursday 20: Harold Graham makes the first test flight of a jetpack, known as the Bell Rocket Belt.

Friday 21: A military coup begins in Algeria, with the intention of preventing the colony becoming independent from France.

Saturday 22: All flights are stopped in Paris and the French army is ordered to resist the Algerian coup.

The Bell Rocket Belt in action.

Sunday 23: French President Charles de Gaulle, although 70 years old and long retired from active service, appears on television in military uniform and declares a State of Emergency following the coup in Algeria.

Monday 24: The Swedish warship *Vasa*, which sunk in 1628, is successfully raised in the Baltic Sea for preservation in a museum in Stockholm.

The 17th century warship *Vasa* arrives in Stockholm after being raised from the sea bed.

April 1961

Tuesday 25: A US patent is granted for the first integrated circuit, an essential component in the development of micro-computers and mobile phones.

France hastily destroys the arming components of its nuclear missiles to prevent the leaders of the Algerian coup from using them.

Wednesday 26: The French coup in Algeria ends with the surrender of most of the mutineers; two generals disappear and form a secret organisation to maintain French rule in the colony.

Thursday 27: Sierra Leone becomes an independent state within the British Commonwealth, with Sir Maurice Dorman as Governor-General.

Friday 28: The final test launch of NASA's manned Mercury rocket takes place.

General Raoul Salan, one of the leaders of the Algerian coup.

Saturday 29: Luciano Pavarotti, 25, makes his operatic debut in La boheme at Reggio Emilia, Italy.

Sunday 30: Eastern Air Lines launches the Eastern Air Shuttle, a no reservation required hourly flight service between New York, Boston and Washington.

May 1961

Monday 1: Betting shops are legalised in the UK.

Tuesday 2: The UK joins the Organisation for Economic Cooperation and Development (OECD).

Wednesday 3: Disgraced British diplomat George Blake is jailed for 42 years for passing secrets to the Soviets.

Thursday 4: Commander Malcolm Ross and Lt Commander Victor A Prather set a new altitude record when they reach 113,740 ft (34.67km) in a balloon. Tragically, Prather drowns during recovery after landing in the Gulf of Mexico.

Friday 5: Alan Shepard becomes the first American in space as the Mercury rocket *Freedom 7* reaches a height of 115 miles, returning to earth 19 minutes later.

Saturday 6: Tottenham Hotspur beats Leicester City 2-0 to win the FA Cup Final at Wembley. Carry Black, ridden by Johnny Sellers wins the Kentucky Derby.

Actor George Clooney is born in Lexington, Kentucky.

George Clooney.

May 1961

Sunday 7: Communist China allows the individual preparation of food instead of compulsory attendance at communal soup kitchens, the inefficiency of which is thought to have contributed to famine in 1958.

Actor Gary Cooper dies on 13 May.

Monday 8: The name of New York's new baseball team is officially announced as the New York Mets. Other names considered were the Avengers, Skyscrapers and Burros.

Tuesday 9: NASA's unmanned test rocket RM-89 *Blue Scout* is destroyed after going off course shortly after launch.

Wednesday 10: 79 people are killed when Air France Flight 406 crashes in the Sahara Desert.

Charles Swart, Governor General of South Africa, is sworn in as the first President as the country leaves the British Commonwealth.

Thursday 11: French President Charles de Gaulle reaffirms his objective to produce nuclear weapons in the Sahara, following the disabling of the programme when it was thought at risk during the recent coup.

Charles Swart becomes the first President of South Africa on 10 May.

Friday 12: The Californian home of Aldous Huxley (author of *Brave New World*) is burnt down during a brush fire, destroying nearly all his unpublished works.

Saturday 13: Hollywood actor Gary Cooper dies aged 60.

May 1961

Guildford Cathedral is consecrated on 18 May.

Sunday 14: British motor racing driver Stirling Moss wins the Monaco Grand Prix.

Monday 15: Pope John Paul XXIII publishes the encyclical *Mater et Magistra*, on the topic of Christianity and social progress.

Tuesday 16: A military coup in South Korea overthrows the government of Prime Minister John M Chang.

President Kennedy of the USA injures his back during a tree planting ceremony in Canada, returning home on crutches.

Wednesday 17: Irish singer and composer Enya (Eithne Patricia Ní Bhraonáin) is born in Gweedore, County Donegal.

Guildford Cathedral near London, England, is consecrated.

Thursday 18: *The Long Absence* and *Viridiana* are jointly awarded the *Palme d'Or* at the 14th Cannes Film Festival.

Friday 19: Soviet probe Venera becomes the first man-made object to fly past another planet, as it reaches Venus.

Saturday 20: The 44th *Giro d'Italia* bicycle race begins in Italy.

Singer Nick Heyward of 1980s band Haircut 100 is born in Beckenham, London.

Pope John Paul XXIII.

May 1961

British Formula One champion Roy Salvadori.

Sunday 21: Martial law is declared in the city of Montgomery, Alabama, after race-riots break out.

Monday 22: Britain's Roy Salvadori wins the London Trophy F1 motor race in a Cooper T53.

Tuesday 23: Nelson Mandela writes to the South African leader of the opposition strongly protesting against leaving the British Commonwealth.

Wednesday 24: 18 people are killed when a USAF Douglas C-124 aircraft crashes near McChord Air Force base, Washington.

Thursday 25: US President John F Kennedy announces that the nation should commit itself to landing a man on the moon by the end of the decade.

Friday 26: *Firefly,* a USAF B-58 bomber, flies from Washington, DC to Paris, France, in a record 3 hours 39 minutes.

May 1961

President and Mrs Kennedy with President de Gaulle of France.

Saturday 27: Tunku Abdul Rahman, Prime Minister of the former British colony of Malaya, announces his plan to form the Federation of Malaysia with neighbouring countries.

Sunday 28: British lawyer Peter Benenson publishes an article in *The Observer* about the plight of political prisoners in Portugal, which leads directly to the founding of human rights group Amnesty International.

Monday 29: The first welfare food stamps are issued in the USA.

Tuesday 30: The first Indianapolis 500 motor race to not be included in the Formula One championship is won by AJ Foyt.

Wednesday 31: US President John F Kennedy and French President Charles de Gaulle meet in Paris, with Jackie Kennedy making her first trip to Europe as First Lady.

June 1961

Thursday 1: Britain's Bradshaw railway timetables, continuously in print since 1839, are published for the last time.

WGFM in New York becomes the first radio station to broadcast on the FM band, on 99.5 Mhz.

Friday 2: SS *Canberra*, the largest British liner to be built since the Second World War, departs from Southampton on its maiden voyage to Australia.

Saturday 3: US President John F Kennedy and Soviet premier Nikita Krushchev meet for summit talks in Vienna, Austria; Krushchev is hostile and demands that US forces leave Berlin.

Sunday 4: The Berlin Crisis begins as the USSR declares that all access routes to and from the US, British and French sectors of West Berlin will be blocked in December.

Monday 5: The United States Supreme Court upholds the legality of the

The psychiatrist Carl Jung dies on 6 June.

June 1961

SS *Canberra* in Sydney Harbour, Australia.

McCarran Act, requiring all US Communist Party members to register with the Justice Department.

Tuesday 6: Swiss psychiatrist Carl Jung, famous for his work on the 'collective unconscious' and religious symbolism, dies aged 85.

Wednesday 7: The Sony Corporation sells its first public stock in the USA.

Thursday 8: Ramon Mercader, released from a 20 year prison term in Mexico for the murder of Soviet dissident Leon Trotsky, is awarded the Order of Lenin in Moscow.

Friday 9: Hollywood actor Michael J Fox is born in Edmonton, Ontario, Canada.

Saturday 10: Two US Army privates, George York and James Latham, are arrested in Utah after murdering seven people while AWOL from Fort Hood, Texas. Both men are later executed.

Actor Michael J Fox is born on 9 June.

June 1961

Singer Boy George is born on 14 June.

Sunday 11: The USA's Phil Hill and Belgium's Olivier Gendebien win the 24 Hours of Le Mans road race in a Ferrari 250 with a record average speed of 115mph.

Monday 12: Ethnically German terrorists blow up 37 electricity pylons in Italy's South Tyrol region; the area is granted autonomy in 1971.

Tuesday 13: British transport union leader Bob Crow is born in Epping, Essex (died 2014).

Wednesday 14: Britain's Department of Transport launches the 'Panda' crossing, a push-button controlled pedestrian crossing. It proves unpopular and is replaced by the 'Pelican' crossing in 1969.

The singer Boy George is born in Bexley, Kent.

Thursday 15: The East German government announces it has no plans to build a wall between East and West Berlin. Construction of the wall begins in August.

Friday 16: While on tour in Europe, Russian ballerin Rudolf Nyureyev defects to the west after a dramatic break for freedom at Le Bourget airport in Paris.

Saturday 17: India's first jet plane, the H-24 Marut, goes into service.

Sunday 18: 32 people are killed when a group opposed to independence for French Algeria bombs a Paris to Strasbourg express train.

The singer Alison Moyet is born in Billericay, Essex.

June 1961

The Carvair car ferry aeroplane goes into service on 21 June.

Monday 19: The British protectorate of Kuwait becomes independent.

Tuesday 20: Following the case for the prosecution in the trial of former Nazi Adolf Eichmann, Eichmann takes the stand, conducting his own defence.

Wednesday 21: The 'Carvair' car ferry aeroplane, developed by British flying entrepreneur Freddie Laker, goes into service.

Thursday 22: Representatives of the three warring factions in Laos, a former colony of French Indochina, meet in neutral Switzerland to agree an armistice.

Friday 23: Major Robert M White USAF becomes the first pilot to travel faster than one mile per second (3,600 mph).

Saturday 24: Henry Miller's novel *Tropic of Cancer* is banned for obscenity in the USA.

Singer Alison Moyet is born on 18 June.

June 1961

Sunday 25: Iraqi President Abdul Karim Kassem announces his country's plans to annexe neighbouring Kuwait, newly independent from Britain. The plan is thwarted when British troops arrive to prevent invasion.

Monday 26: African National Congress leader Nelson Mandela goes into hiding in South Africa to avoid arrest.

Tuesday 27: Arthur Michael Ramsey is ordained as the 100th Archbishop of Canterbury, worldwide leader of the Anglican church.

Wednesday 28: The John Ford western film *Two Rode Together* starring James Stewart and Richard Widmark is released in the USA.

Thursday 29: The first break-up of a satellite in orbit takes place when a NASA Thor-Able rocket explodes 600 miles above Earth.

Arthur Michael Ramsay becomes the Archbishop of Canterbury on 27 July.

Friday 30: US inventor Lee De Forest, who designed the first amplifying vacuum tube (an essential component for radios) dies aged 87.

July 1961

Saturday 1: Lady Diana Spencer (later Diana, Princess of Wales) is born in Sandringham, Norfolk (died 1997).

Sunday 2: Novelist Ernest Hemingway commits suicide aged 61.

Monday 3: Edwin Perkins, inventor of the soft drink Kool-Aid, dies aged 72.

Attempted suicide is de-criminalised in England and Wales.

Tuesday 4: Barclay's Bank in Drummond Street, London NW1, becomes the first British bank to use a computer (an EMI Mainframe) in-house.

Diana, Princess of Wales, is born on 1 August.

Wednesday 5: Israel launches its first space rocket, Shavit 2.

Thursday 6: North Korea and the USSR sign a treaty of mutual co-operation.

Friday 7: Australia's Rod Laver defeats the USA's Chuck McKinley to win the men's Wimbledon tennis final.

July 1961

Wimbledon tennis champion Rod Laver signs autographs for young fans.

Saturday 8: Angela Mortimer beats Christine Trueman, both of Britain, at the Wimbledon Ladies' Singles tennis championships; it is the first time a British woman has won the title since 1937.

Sunday 9: Greece becomes an associate member of the Common Market (later the European Union).

Monday 10: The top selling single of 1961 in the USA, *Tossin' and Turnin'* by Bobby Lewis, hits number one in the charts.

Tuesday 11: The English version of Jean Anouilh's play *Becket,* about the murder of St Thomas A Becket, opens in London starring Eric Porter, Christopher Plummer and Diana Rigg.

Wednesday 12: The USA's Tiros-3 satellite is launched, and takes the first photographs of a storm from orbit.

Thursday 13: Psychiatrist Robert Soblen, a US citizen of Lithuanian origin, is convicted of spying for the Russians and sentenced to life imprisonment. He later flees to Israel and commits suicide in 1962.

Friday 14: Huge crowds turn out to greet returning cosmonaut Major Yuri Gagarin as he visits London, where he attends a state luncheon with Queen Elizabeth II.

July 1961

Saturday 15: German racing driver Wolfgang Von Trips wins the 1961 British Grand Prix at Aintree.

Sunday 16: Seven people are killed and 116 injured in a railway crash at Singleton Bank in Lancashire, England.

Wolfgang von Trips on the racing circuit.

Monday 17: Valery Brumel of the USSR sets a new high jump record of 7' 4" (2.24 metres).

Legendary baseball player Ty Cobb dies aged 74.

Tuesday 18: A plan by the Basque separatist group ETA to blow up a train is foiled by Spanish authorities.

Wednesday 19: The first regular in-flight movie service begins on TWA flights between New York and Los Angeles.

Thursday 20: The Arab League votes to admit Kuwait as a member and to send troops to relieve the British force on guard against Iraqi invasion.

Friday 21: Gus Grissom becomes the second American in space, as he reaches a height of 118 miles in the Liberty Bell 7 capsule.

Gus Grissom and the Liberty Bell.

July 1961

Saturday 22: The British government agrees to pay the small European kingdom of San Marino £80,000 in compensation for war damage mistakenly caused by RAF bombers attacking Italy during the Second World War.

Sunday 23: American actor Woody Harrelson is born in Midland, Texas.

Monday 24: Eastern Airlines flight 202 is hijacked after take-off from Miami and ordered to fly to Cuba by Cuban born US citizen Wilfred Oquendo.

Tuesday 25: US President John F Kennedy makes a nationwide broadcast stating that he is prepared to go to war with the Soviet Union if the Russians attempt to seize West Berlin.

The crime thriller *Whistle Down the Wind* starring John Mills and his daughter Hayley is released in the UK.

Wednesday 26: Southern Rhodesia (now Zimbabwe) introduces a limited number of seats for black MPs in its formerly all-white Parliament.

Thursday 27: Mock auctions are banned in the UK.

Friday 28: A declassified CIA document on this day shows that Britain seriously considered withdrawal of troops from its colony of Hong Kong to save money. The withdrawal does not take place until 1997.

Saturday 29: The value of Pi is calculated to 100,000 places for the first time, by researchers Daniel Shanks and John Wrench using an IBM 7090 computer in New York.

Sunday 30: The USSR publishes a twenty year plan predicting free housing, utilities and food by 1980.

Monday 31: The USSR announces the end of a three-year moratorium on nuclear testing.

August 1961

Tuesday 1: East Germany begins restricting traffic into West Berlin.

Wednesday 2: 16 American tourists are killed when their tour bus crashes into Lake Lucerne in Switzerland.

Thursday 3: The nuclear submarine USS *Thresher* is commissioned.

Friday 4: Barack Obama, 44th President of the USA, is born in Honolulu, Hawaii.

Saturday 5: In the Berlin Crisis, the countries of the Warsaw Pact agree that all US, British and French occupying forces must leave West Berlin. Thousands of people begin fleeing from East to West Berlin.

Barack Obama is born on 4 August.

Sunday 6: Soviet cosmonaut Gherman Titov becomes the first person to sleep in space and, at 25, the youngest person in space, a record that still stands in 2020.

Monday 7: The Milgram Experiment begins at Yale University, where participants are ordered to give electric shocks to other

August 1961

volunteers in order to test people's willingness to obey orders from authority.

Tuesday 8: The first issue of the Marvel superhero comic *The Fantastic Four* is published.

Queen Elizabeth II makes the first state visit of a British sovereign to Northern Ireland since 1690.

Wednesday 9: 39 Britons, most of them schoolboys, are killed when their chartered plane crashes in Norway.

James Benton Parsons becomes the first black district judge in the USA.

Thursday 10: The United Kingdom applies for membership of the European Economic Community (later the EU). The application is vetoed by France in 1963 but the UK eventually joins in 1975.

Friday 11: The former Portuguese colonies of Dadra and Nagar Haveli are brought under the control of India.

East German volunteer reserve troops close off the border into West Berlin on 13 August.

August 1961

The Bell UH-1D helicopter is first flown on 16 August.

Saturday 12: East Germany signs the order to close off West Berlin; a record 2,662 East Berliners manage to flee to the west on this day.

Sunday 13: Construction of the Berlin Wall begins at 2.00 am with the erection of a temporary barbed wire fence, troop cordons and the closure of road and rail crossings.

Monday 14: Kenyan nationalist leader Jomo Kenyatta is released from prison and returns to a rapturous welcome in the capital, Nairobi. He becomes the country's first Prime Minister after independence from Britain in 1963.

Tuesday 15: India's Sikh leader Tara Singh Malhotra begins a six week hunger strike as part of a campaign for a Sikh state; the Indian government agrees to this in 1966.

Wednesday 16: The US Army's primary helicopter in the Vietnam War, the Bell UH-1D, is flown for the first time.

Thursday 17: The US government approves the use of the oral polio vaccine, replacing the previous injected vaccine.

Friday 18: The construction of the permanent Berlin Wall begins.

August 1961

Saturday 19: Professor Timothy Leary at Harvard University delivers his first paper on the use of the hallucinogenic drug LSD.

Sunday 20: A convoy of 100 trucks and 1500 US troops is sent to reinforce the Allied garrisons of West Berlin.

Monday 21: Francisco Goya's 1812 portrait of the Duke of Wellington is stolen from London's National Gallery. It is finally recovered in a Birmingham railway station in 1965.

Tuesday 22: Mrs Ida Siekmann, 58, becomes the first person to die while crossing the Berlin Wall, after attempting to jump over from the third floor of a nearby house.

Goya's portrait of the Duke of Wellington is stolen on 21 August.

Wednesday 23: In the notorious case known as the A6 Murder, Michael Gregsten is murdered in a lay-by in Bedfordshire, England, and his companion Valerie Story is left for dead. James Hanratty is eventually convicted of the killing and executed in 1962.

Thursday 24: Gunter Litfin, 24, becomes the first person to be shot dead by border guards while attempting to cross the Berlin Wall.

Friday 25: Jacqueline Thomas, 15, is found murdered in Alum Rock, Birmingham, England. A nationwide manhunt follows but the killer is not identified until 2007.

Saturday 26: Buddhism is declared the official religion of Burma.

The Hockey Hall of Fame opens in Toronto, Canada.

August 1961

Sunday 27: Britain's Stirling Moss wins the 1961 Danish Grand Prix motor race.

Fashion designer Tom Ford is born in Austin, Texas.

Monday 28: UN peacekeeping troops carry out Operation Rum Punch to put down a secessionist uprising in the former Belgian Congo.

Tuesday 29: The first group of US Peace Corps volunteers departs for Ghana.

Wednesday 30: Racial segregation in schools in Atlanta, Georgia, ends peaceably.

Thursday 31: The film *Victim*, starring Dirk Bogarde, premieres in the UK. It is the first film to openly mention homosexuality.

President Kennedy (left) addresses members of the Peace Corps before they depart for service in Ghana.

September 1961

Friday 1: 78 people are killed when TWA Flight 529 crashes near Chicago. It is the worst US air disaster to this date.

Saturday 2: The Brazilian government adopts a parliamentary system; it lasts for only 16 months.

Sunday 3: The UK and USA propose a tripartite moratorium on nuclear testing with the USSR; the Soviets initially refuse but agree in 1963.

Monday 4: Richard Nixon makes a hole in one while playing golf at Bel-Air Country Club in California. He and Gerald Ford are the only US presidents to have achieved this feat.

Tuesday 5: Aeroplane hijacking, or 'skyjacking' is made a federal crime in the USA punishable by up to 20 years imprisonment or in some cases, execution.

Wednesday 6: The secure telephone line between Washington DC and London is set up, to enable the US President and British Prime Minister to speak directly to each other.

Thursday 7: Writers Richard Maibaum and Wolf Mankewicz begin work on the screenplay for the first James Bond film, *Dr No*.

September 1961

The last London Underground steam engines are withdrawn from passenger service on 9 September.

Friday 8: An attempted assassination of French President Charles de Gaulle takes place when a roadside bomb fails to blow up his car near Colombey-les-Deux-Eglises.

The world's most successful series of sci-fi novels, *Perry Rhodan*, with nearly 5000 novels published, begins in Germany.

Saturday 9: The last steam hauled passenger trains on the London Underground are taken out of service. Steam shunting locomotives remain in service on the network until 1971.

Sunday 10: Formula One driver Wolfgang Von Trips of Germany and Canadian hydroplane driver Bob Hayward, both aged 33, are both killed in separate racing accidents on this day.

Monday 11: The international non-governmental environment body The World Wildlife Fund is set up.

Tuesday 12: Five days before training is due to begin, the USA's female astronaut programme is cancelled. The first American woman does not go into space until 1983.

September 1961

Wednesday 13: The US Army presents its top secret plans for nuclear war to President Kennedy. The plan includes dropping over 3000 nuclear bombs on Russia and China in the event of war being declared.

Thursday 14: The film *A Taste of Honey* starring Rita Tushingham is released in the UK.

Friday 15: The 61st US Amateur Golf Championship is won by 21-year-old Jack Nicklaus.

Saturday 16: Three people are killed and 35 injured when a spectator stand collapses at Ibrox Park football stadium in Glasgow, Scotland.

Sunday 17: Police arrest 1300 Campaign for Nuclear Disarmament protestors during a demonstration in Trafalgar Square, London.

Monday 18: The UN Secretary-General Dag Hammarskjöld is killed in a plane crash while travelling to negotiate a cease fire with rebels in the Congo.

UN Secretary General Dag Hammarskjöld is killed on 18 September.

Tuesday 19: One of the first reported cases of alien abduction is alleged to have occurred as Barney and Betty Hill claim to have been taken aboard a UFO near Lancaster, New Hampshire.

Wednesday 20: The CIA moves to its new headquarters in Langley, Virginia.

Thursday 21: Pro-independence terrorists blow up Algeria's main TV transmitter moments before it is due to broadcast a speech by French President Charles de Gaulle.

Earle Dickson, inventor of the 'Band Aid' sticking plaster, dies aged 68.

September 1961

Friday 22: Antonio Abertondo of Argentina becomes the first person to swim across the English Channel and back again, resting for only ten minutes between the 21 mile crossings.

Saturday 23: NBC TV launches *Saturday Night at the Movies*, showing relatively recent colour films. Previously most films shown on TV were at least 12 years old.

Jackie Gleason as Minnesota Fats in *The Hustler*.

Sunday 24: Walt Disney's *Wonderful World of Color* documentary series premieres on NBC TV; it is credited with hugely increasing sales of colour TV sets in the USA.

Monday 25: Wisconsin becomes the first US state to require the fitting of seatbelts on all new vehicles.

The film *The Hustler* starring Paul Newman and Jackie Gleason is released.

Tuesday 26: The international governing body for association football, FIFA, suspends South Africa from international competitions due to its apartheid policy.

Wednesday 27: Sierra Leone becomes the 100th member of the United Nations.

The cartoon series *Top Cat* is launched in the US.

Top Cat.

Thursday 28: The word 'ain't' officially enters the English language, appearing in the new edition of Webster's Dictionary.

September 1961

The stars of *Dr Kildare* (*from left*) Richard Chamberlain, Daniella Bianchi and Raymond Massey.

Friday 29: Soviet premier Nikita Kruschev writes a conciliatory letter to US President Kennedy, asking for a peaceful resolution to the Berlin Crisis.

The medical drama serial *Dr Kildare* starring Richard Chamberlain first airs on US TV.

Saturday 30: 20 year olds John Lennon and Paul McCartney begin a hitch-hiking trip through France, wearing bowler hats to attract the attention of motorists.

October 1961

Sunday 1: The BBC broadcasts the first episode of its long-running religious programme *Songs of Praise*.

Monday 2: French President Charles de Gaulle delivers a speech on French and Algerian television, stating his plan to allow Algerians self-determination.

Tuesday 3: *The Dick Van Dyke* show airs on US TV for the first time.

The Motion Picture Association of America changes its guidelines to allow homosexuality in films to be suggested, although not openly mentioned.

Dick Van Dyke with his on-screen wife, Mary Tyler Moore.

Wednesday 4: The *Fianna Fail* party led by Sean Lemass wins the Irish general election.

Thursday 5: The film *Breakfast at Tiffany's* starring Audrey Hepburn and George Peppard is released.

October 1961

On 7 October, Willy Finder and his four year old son Michael escape from East to West Berlin by jumping from a four-storey building. The picture shows the dramatic moment of Michael *(circled)* jumping while firemen wait to catch him in a blanket.

Friday 6: The East German army are given the formal order to shoot any persons attempting to cross the Berlin Wall.

Saturday 7: 34 British tourists are killed when a Douglas Dakota of Derby Aviation crashes in the French Pyrenees.

Sunday 8: East Berlin residents begin to escape to the west via the sewers under the Berlin Wall. At least 134 people manage to flee before the route is discovered by police.

Monday 9: The New York Yankees beat the Cincinatti Reds 13-5 to win baseball's World Series.

Tuesday 10: Following a volcanic eruption, all 260 residents of the tiny British colony of Tristan da Cunha in the Atlantic ocean are evacuated to England, where they remain for two years.

Wednesday 11: Major Robert White USAF flies an X-15 fighter to a height of 40 miles, 8 miles higher than the previous record.

Chico Marx, eldest of the Marx Brothers comedians, dies aged 74.

Thursday 12: New Zealand abolishes the death penalty.

October 1961

Friday 13: Prince Louis Rwagasore, heir to throne of Burundi, is assassinated.

Saturday 14: All commercial flights in the USA and Canada are grounded for 12 hours for the military aerial defence exercise Operation Skyshield II.

Sunday 15: Mickey Wright wins the LPGA Women's Golf Tournament.

Monday 16: Culinary writer Julia Child's first bestselling book *Mastering the Art of French Cooking* is published.

Julia Child.

Tuesday 17: 140 people are killed and over 11,000 arrested in Paris as Algerian Muslim immigrants protest over curfew rules. Police chief Maurice Papon is eventually tried for the massacre in 1988.

Wednesday 18: The musical film *West Side Story* premieres in New York; it goes on to win ten Academy Awards.

Jazz musician Wynton Marsalis is born in New Orleans, Louisiana.

Thursday 19: The last British troops leave the newly independent Gulf state of Kuwait.

Friday 20: The first live nuclear missile is launched from a submarine, during Soviet tests in the Arctic.

Natalie Wood stars in *West Side Story*.

October 1961

Teenagers dance the Twist at an open-air disco in Berlin, Germany.

Saturday 21: *U1*, the first German submarine built since the end of the Second World War, is launched at Kiel, West Germany.

Sunday 22: Singer Chubby Checker performs The Twist on the *Ed Sullivan Show*, starting a nationwide dance craze.

Monday 23: The US Navy carries out the first successful underwater launch of a Polaris missile from the submarine USS *Ethan Allen* off the Florida coast.

Tuesday 24: Conservationists meet with British Prime Minister Harold MacMillan to try to preserve the Euston Arch, part of London's oldest railway station, from demolition; they are unsuccessful but later save St Pancras Station from a similar fate.

Wednesday 25: Mongolia is admitted to the United Nations.

The first edition of the long-running satirical magazine *Private Eye* is published in London.

Thursday 26: Turkey's General Cemal Gurcel, who seized power in a military coup in 1960, is elected President.

The first issue of *Private Eye* is published on 25 October.

October 1961

Friday 27: In the Berlin Crisis, massed Soviet and US tanks face each other at Checkpoint Charlie in a tense 16 hour stand off.

Saturday 28: US and Soviet tanks begin a gradual withdrawal from Berlin's East/West border.

Sunday 29: Konstantino Karamanlis is elected Prime Minister of Greece.

Monday 30: The largest man-made explosion ever to take place occurs when the Soviets test a 50-megaton hydrogen bomb in Novaya Zemlya, Siberia.

Tuesday 31: 307 people are killed when Hurricane Hattie hits British Honduras (now Belize).

Film director Peter Jackson (*Lord of the Rings*) is born in Pukerua Bay, New Zealand.

Above: the tense stand-off at Checkpoint Charlie on 27 October.

November 1961

Wednesday 1: The US Interstate Commerce Commission bans racial segregation in all interstate facilities such as railway stations and bus terminals.

Thursday 2: Soviet army officer Oleg Penkovsky is caught passing top secret military information to the US and UK. He is executed in 1963.

Friday 3: U Thant is elected Secretary General of the United Nations.

Sean Connery is announced as the actor chosen to play James Bond in the forthcoming film *Dr No*.

Viscount Linley, Earl Snowdon, first child of HRH Princess Margaret and Antony Armstrong-Jones, is born in London.

Sean Connery lands the part of James Bond.

Saturday 4: Actor Ralph Macchio (*The Karate Kid*) is born in Huntingdon, New York.

Britain's Prime Minister rejects calls to preserve London's historic Euston Arch; demolition begins on 7 November.

November 1961

U Thant becomes UN Secretary General on 3 November.

Catch-22 is published on 9 November.

Sunday 5: India's Prime Minister Jawaharlal Nehru makes a state visit to the USA.

Monday 6: Heinz Felfe, chief of West German counterintelligence, is caught passing secrets to the Soviets.

Tuesday 7: France secretly tests its first nuclear bomb underground.

Wednesday 8: US amateur golf champion Jack Nicklaus turns professional.

The majority of Welsh counties vote in a referendum to keep public houses closed on Sundays.

Thursday 9: Rosemarie Frankland becomes the first British Miss World.

Captain Robert White USAF becomes the first pilot to reach Mach 6, flying an X-15 rocket at 4093 mph (6590 kmh).

Friday 10: The Russian city of Stalingrad is renamed Volgograd.

Joseph Heller's best selling novel *Catch-22* is published.

Saturday 11: 13 Italian airmen are killed in an ambush while on UN peacekeeping duties in the former Belgian Congo.

Sunday 12: Retired USAF Captain Julian Harvey sinks the yacht *Bluebelle* in the Bahamas to kill his wife for her life insurance, drowning six other passengers in the process; one is later found alive and, knowing that he will be caught, Harvey commits suicide.

November 1961

Monday 13: One of the biggest fires on record starts at a natural gas well in Algeria; it is eventually stopped by firefighter Red Adair in April 1962.

Tuesday 14: A resolution to expel South Africa from the United Nations is rejected.

Wednesday 15: Former Argentine President Juan Peron marries Isabel Cartas. Following Peron's re-election then death in 1974, Mrs Peron becomes the world's first female President.

Thursday 16: The US military begins the first tactical airlift operations in Vietnam.

Friday 17: The first successful US missile launch from an underground silo takes place at Cape Canaveral, Florida.

Juan Peron and Isabel Cartas are married on 15 November.

Saturday 18: Widukind Lenz of Germany becomes the first doctor to raise concerns about the anti-morning sickness drug Thalidomide, which is later proven to cause serious birth defects in children.

Sunday 19: Michael Rockefeller, 23, son of future US Vice-President Nelson Rockefeller and heir to the Rockefeller fortune, goes missing, presumed dead, while boating in Netherlands New Guinea.

Actress Meg Ryan is born in Fairfield, Connecticut.

Meg Ryan is born on 19 November.

Monday 20: Turkey's first civilian government since its 1960 military coup begins under Prime Minister Ismet Inonu.

November 1961

Tuesday 21: The first revolving restaurant in the USA, La Ronde (later renamed Windows of Hawaii) opens in Honolulu, Hawaii.

Wednesday 22: Robert Bolt's play *A Man for All Seasons*, about the life of St Thomas More, opens on Broadway.

Thursday 23: The anti-morning sickness drug Thalidomide is banned in West Germany following concerns about harmful effects on unborn children.

Cricketer Merv 'The Swerve' Hughes is born in Victoria, Australia.

Ismet Inonu becomes President of Turkey on 20 November.

Friday 24: Axel Wenner-Gren, Swedish inventor of the domestic vacuum cleaner, dies aged 80.

HM Queen Elizabeth II begins a state visit to newly independent Sierra Leone.

Saturday 25: The world's first nuclear powered aircraft carrier, the USS *Enterprise*, is commissioned.

The USS *Enterprise*.

November 1961

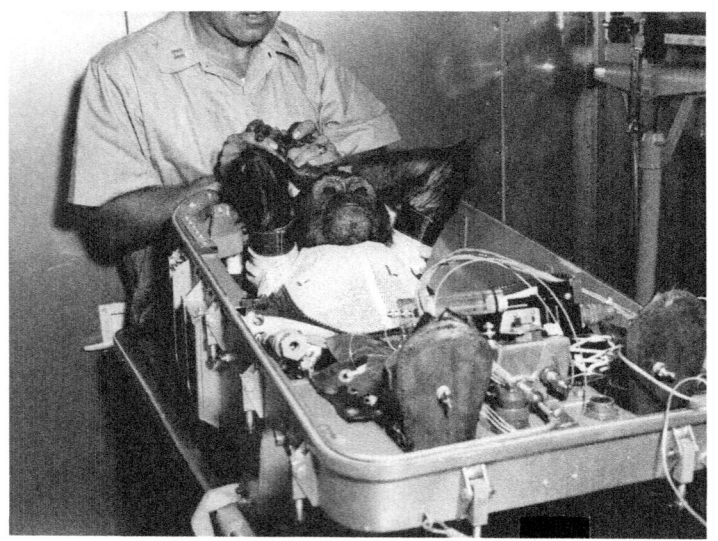

Enos the chimp is prepared for space flight on 29 November.

Sunday 26: World Zionist Organisation leader Israel Cohen dies aged 82.

Monday 27: British actress Samantha Bond (Miss Moneypenny in the James Bond films) is born in London.

Tuesday 28: Israel begins Operation Yachin, the secret repatriation of Moroccan Jews to Israel.

Wednesday 29: Enos the chimpanzee is launched into space from Cape Canaveral on board Mercury-Atlas 5, as a test flight for the first American man to be sent into orbit.

Thursday 30: The US government begins Operation Mongoose, the secret attempt to overthrow Cuban leader Fidel Castro.

December 1961

Friday 1: The Dutch colony of Netherlands New Guinea is granted independence as West Papua.

Saturday 2: Cuban leader Fidel Castro announces that all political parties (except his) are to be banned.

Sunday 3: After 47 days on public display to over 116,000 visitors, staff at New York's Museum of Modern art discover that an abstract painting by Henri Matisse is hanging upside down.

Monday 4: Boxer Floyd Patterson (USA) defeats Tom McNeeley in Toronto to retain the World Heavyweight title.

Boxer Floyd Patterson retains the World Heavyweight title on 4 December.

US troops in Vietnam begin a programme of jungle deforestation.

Tuesday 5: The largest ever mass escape from East Berlin to the west takes place when railwayman Harry Deterling drives 19 people on a train through the border on a little-used branch line; the authorities rip the tracks up the next day.

December 1961

Sir Robert Menzies becomes Prime Minister of Australia on 9 December.

Wednesday 6: NASA announces that the USA will put a man (John Glenn) into space orbit in 1962.

Thursday 7: British and Norwegian explorers celebrate the fiftieth anniversary of the conquest of the South Pole with the presentation at the Pole of a signed photo from Olav Bjaaland, 88, the last survivor of the 1911 expedition.

Friday 8: The Beach Boys (under their original name of The Pendletones) release their first single, *Surfin'*.

Saturday 9: The British colony of Tanganyika is granted independence.

Robert Menzies' Liberal Party is victorious in Australia's general election.

Sunday 10: UN Secretary General Dag Hammarskjold is posthumously awarded the Nobel Peace Prize.

Monday 11: The Vietnam War officially begins for the USA, as 400 troops are sent to Saigon.

At his trial in Israel, Nazi war criminal Adolf Eichmann is found guilty of genocide.

Tuesday 12: 13 men are arrested in Tokyo as police break up a plot to assassinate the Prime Minister, Hayato Ideka.

Senior Nazi Adolf Eichmann is found guilty of genocide, on 11 December.

December 1961

British Prime Minister Harold Macmillan *(left)* and US President Kennedy *(centre)* with Major General Sir Julian Avery Gascoigne, Governor of Bermuda, meet for talks on 21 December.

Wednesday 13: The USA and USSR announce the formation of a joint committee on nuclear disarmament.

American painter Anna Robertson 'Grandma' Moses dies aged 101.

Thursday 14: 20 schoolchildren are killed when their bus is hit by a train on a level crossing near Greeley, Colorado.

Friday 15: Nazi war criminal Adolf Eichmann is sentenced to death.

Saturday 16: The African National Congress begins a bombing campaign in South Africa; leader Nelson Mandela later justifies this by stating that only unoccupied buildings were targetted.

Sunday 17: Robert Mugabe and Joshua Nkomo found the Zimbabwe African Peoples' Union to end white rule in Rhodesia.

Monday 18: The Indian Army invades the Portuguese colony of Goa; the Governor General surrenders the following day, ending 451 years of colonial rule.

December 1961

Tuesday 19: The French space programme, CNES, is set up.

Wednesday 20: Robert McGladdery becomes the last person to be hanged in Northern Ireland.

Thursday 21: US President Kennedy and British Prime Minister Harold Macmillan meet for talks in the British colony of Bermuda.

Friday 22: Sergeant James T Davis of Livingston, Tennessee, becomes the first US serviceman officially announced as a fatality in the Vietnam War.

Saturday 23: 71 people are killed in a train crash in Catanzaro, Italy. The drive is later found to have been travelling at twice the safe speed limit.

Sunday 24: General Francisco Franco, dictator of Spain, is injured during a hunting accident.

The Houston Oilers beat the San Diego Chargers 10-3 to win the 1961 American Football League Championship.

British Formula One champion Jim Clark wins the South African Grand Prix on 26 December.

December 1961

Patrick O'Neal stars in Tennessee Williams' play *The Night of the Iguana*, which opens on 28 December.

Monday 25: Pope John XXIII summons the Second Vatican Council, which leads to dramatic changes in the doctrine and liturgy of the Roman Catholic church.

Tuesday 26: The British racing driver Jim Clark wins the 1961 South African Grand Prix.

Wednesday 27: New York's Empire State Building is sold by the Prudential Insurance Company to a group of investors for $65,000,000 in one of history's most complicated property transactions, requiring 100 legal professionals to carry it out.

Thursday 28: Former US First Lady Edith Wilson dies aged 89.

Tennessee Williams' play *The Night of the Iguana* premieres in New York City, starring Patrick O'Neal and Bette Davis.

Friday 29: French President Charles de Gaulle announces in a televised speech that French rule in Algeria will end in 1962.

Saturday 30: Shostakovich's Fourth Symphony is performed for the first time, at the Moscow Conservatory.

Sunday 31: The Republic of Ireland's first television station, *Telefis Eireann* (later RTE) begins broadcasting, with an address by President Eamon de Valera.

Printed in Great Britain
by Amazon